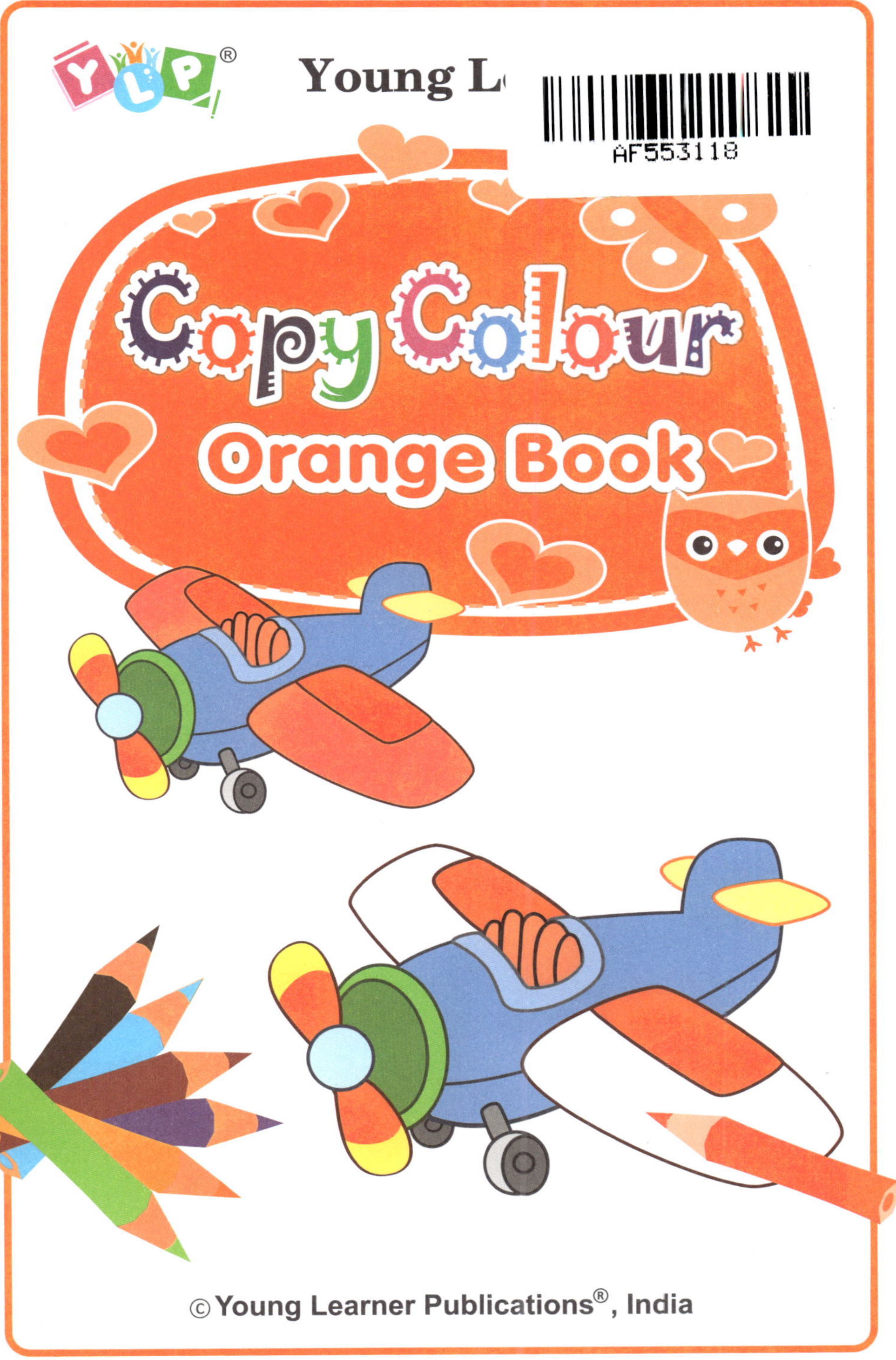

YLP
Young L
AF553118
Copy Colour
Orange Book

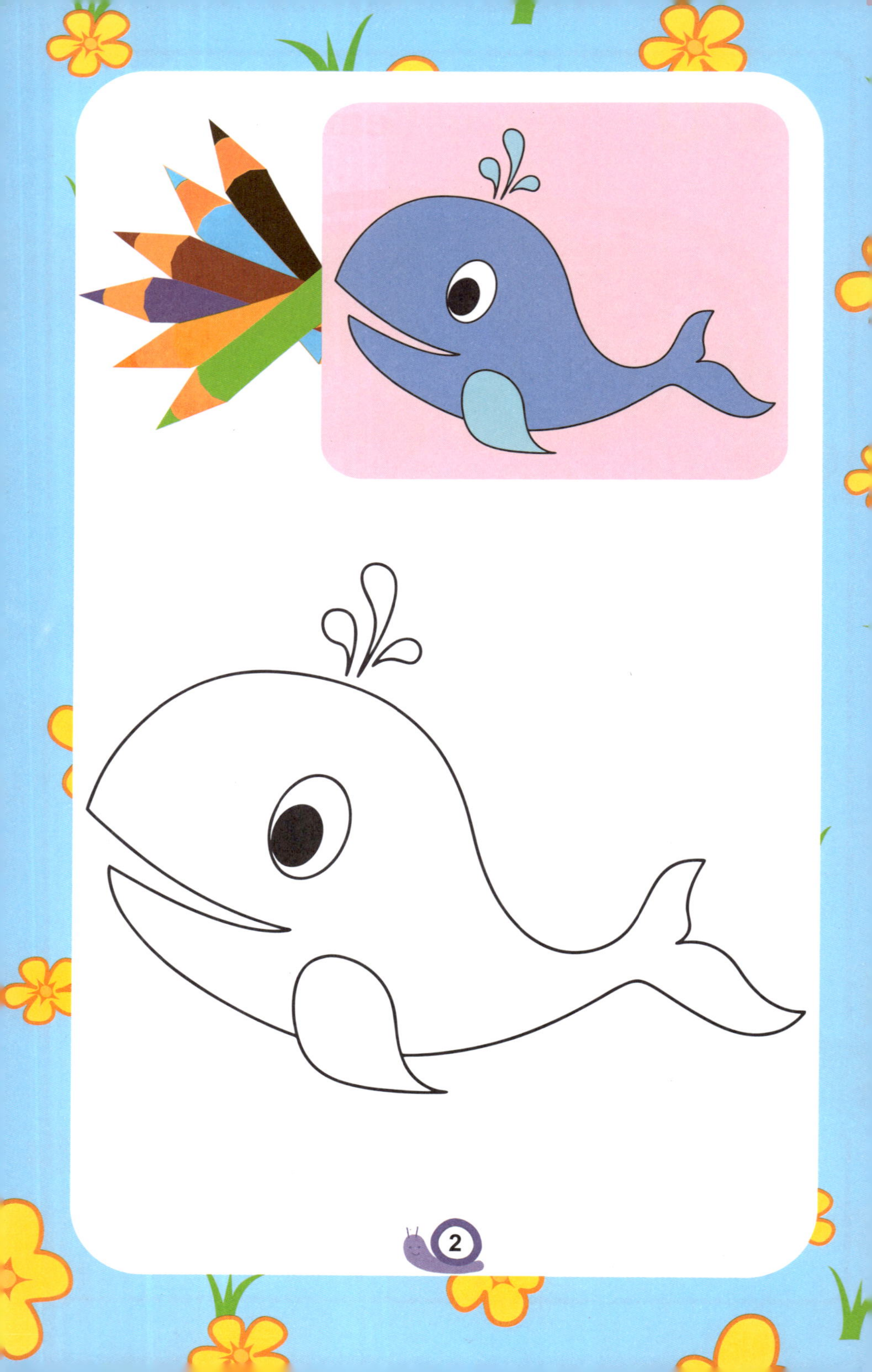

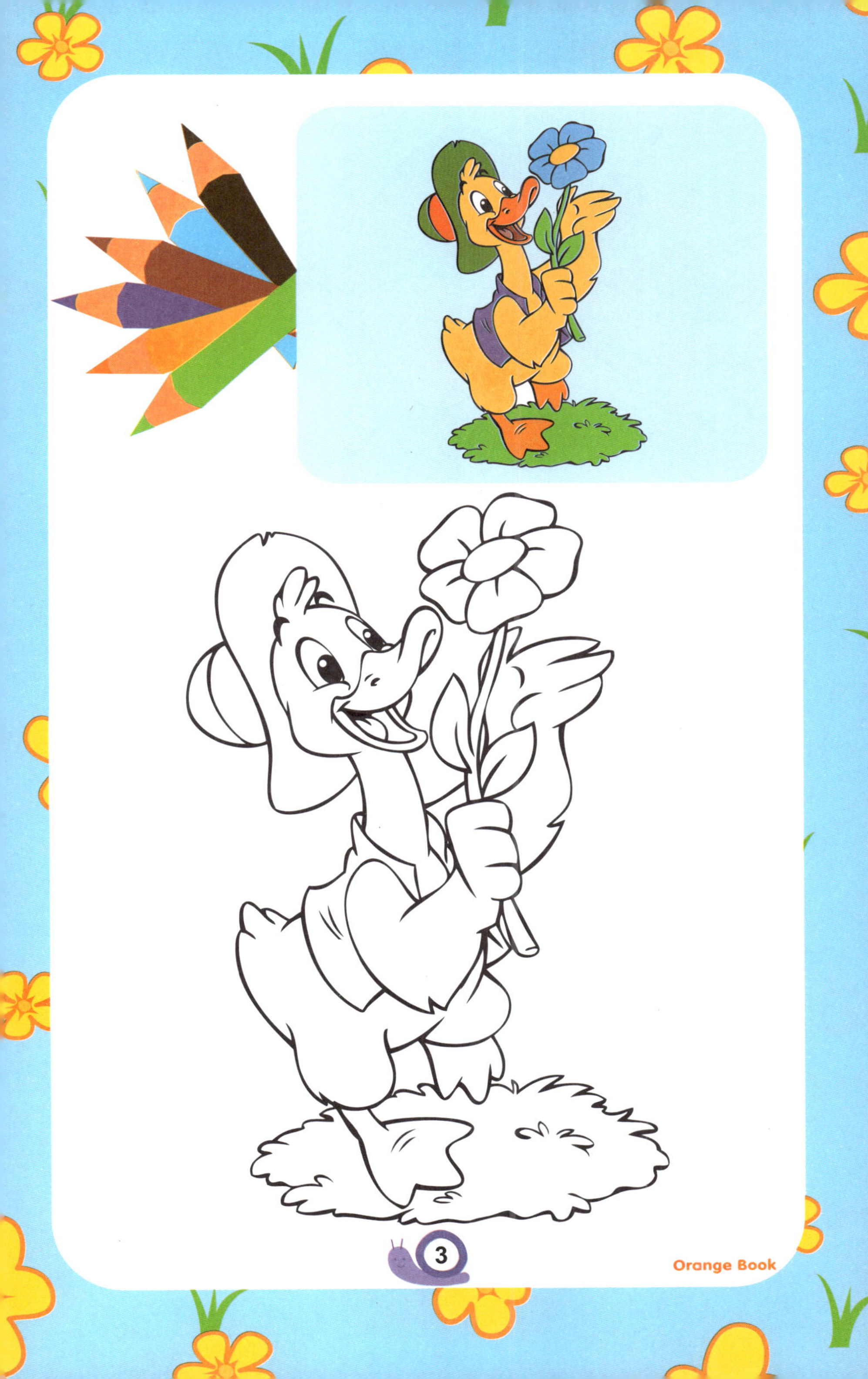

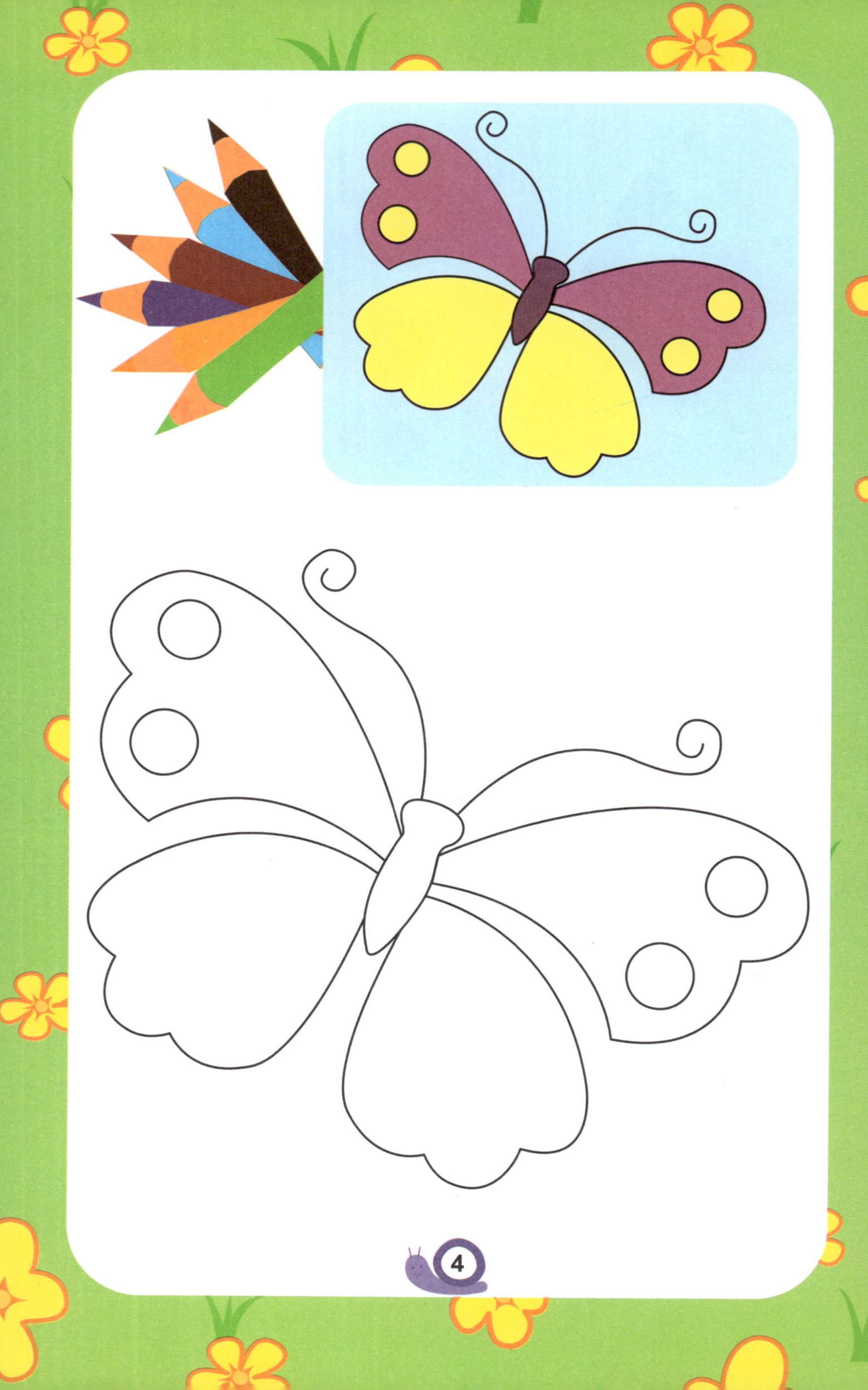

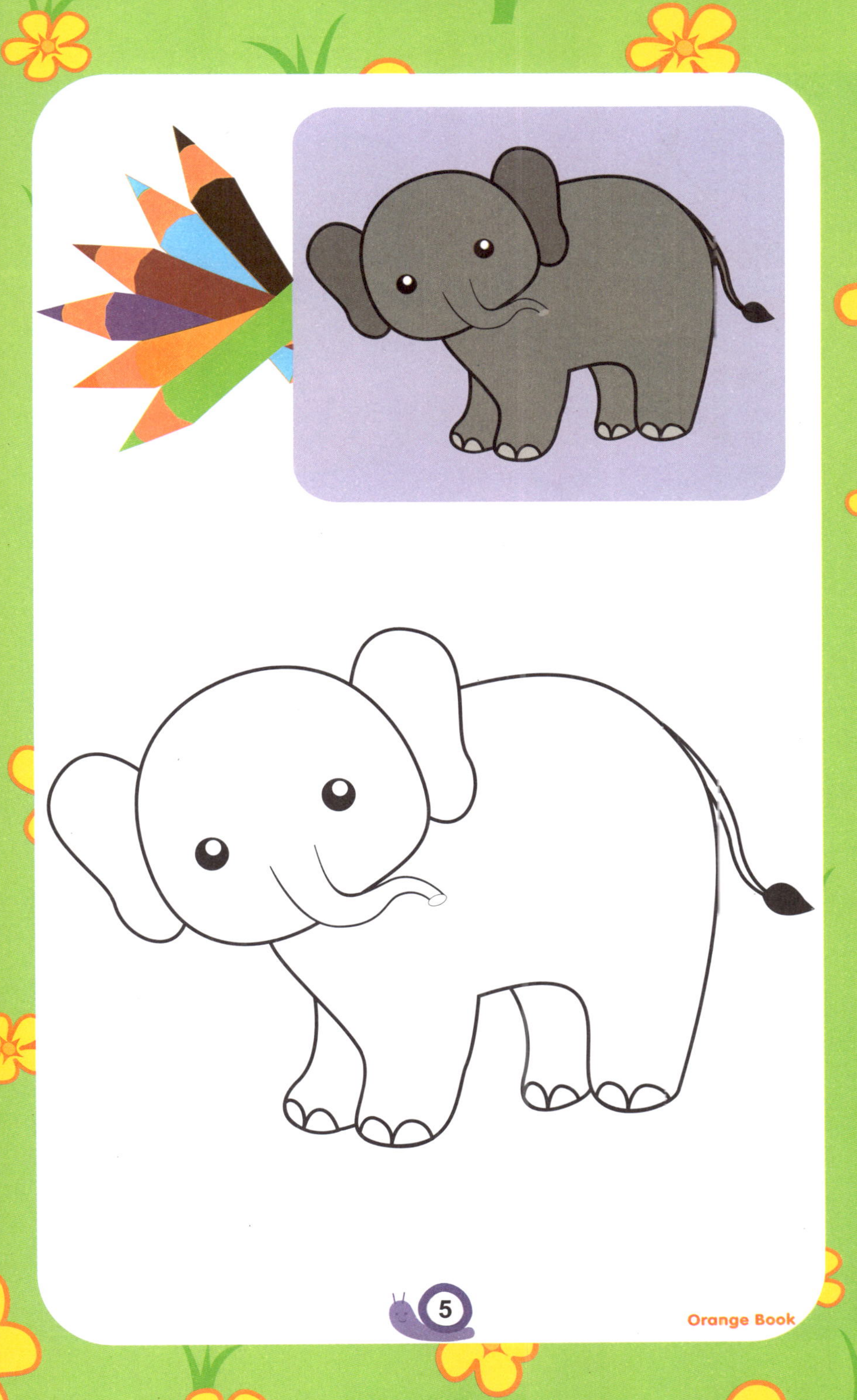

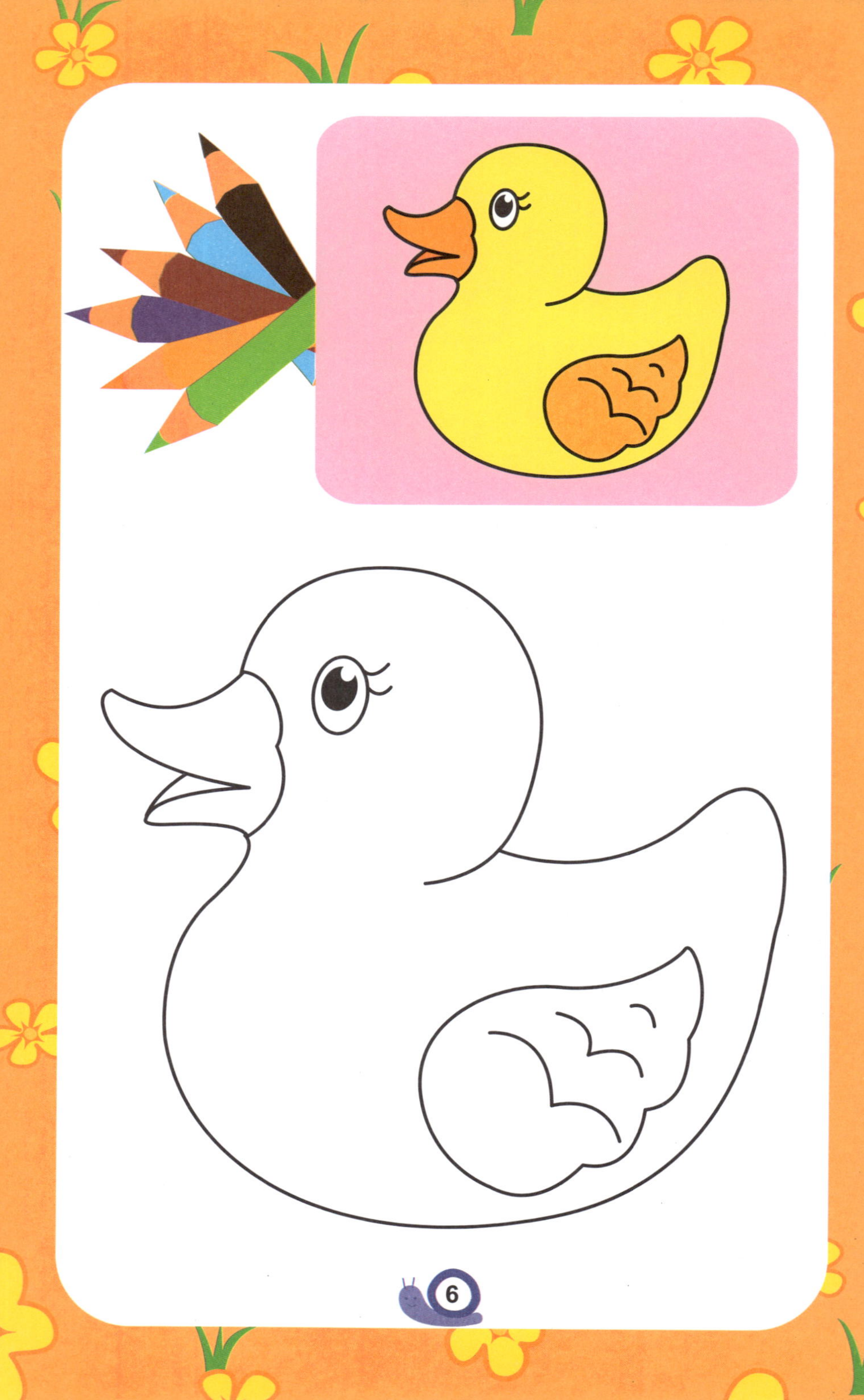

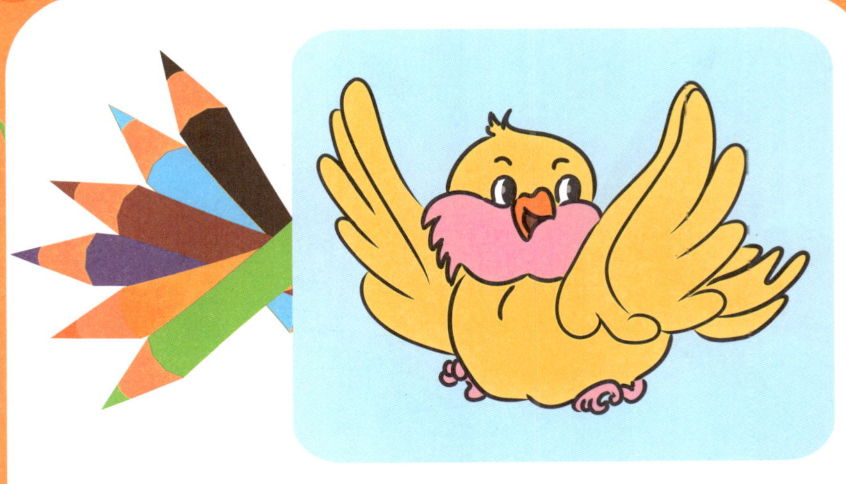

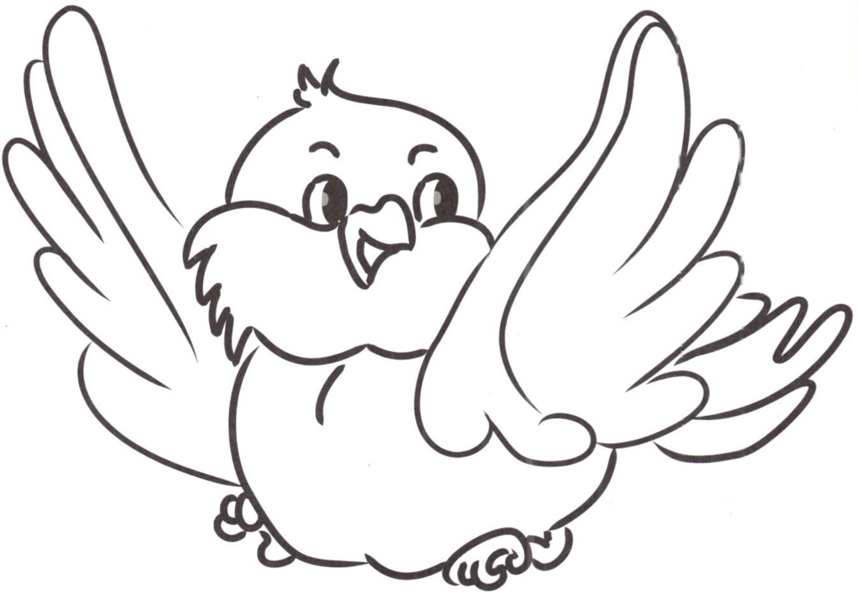

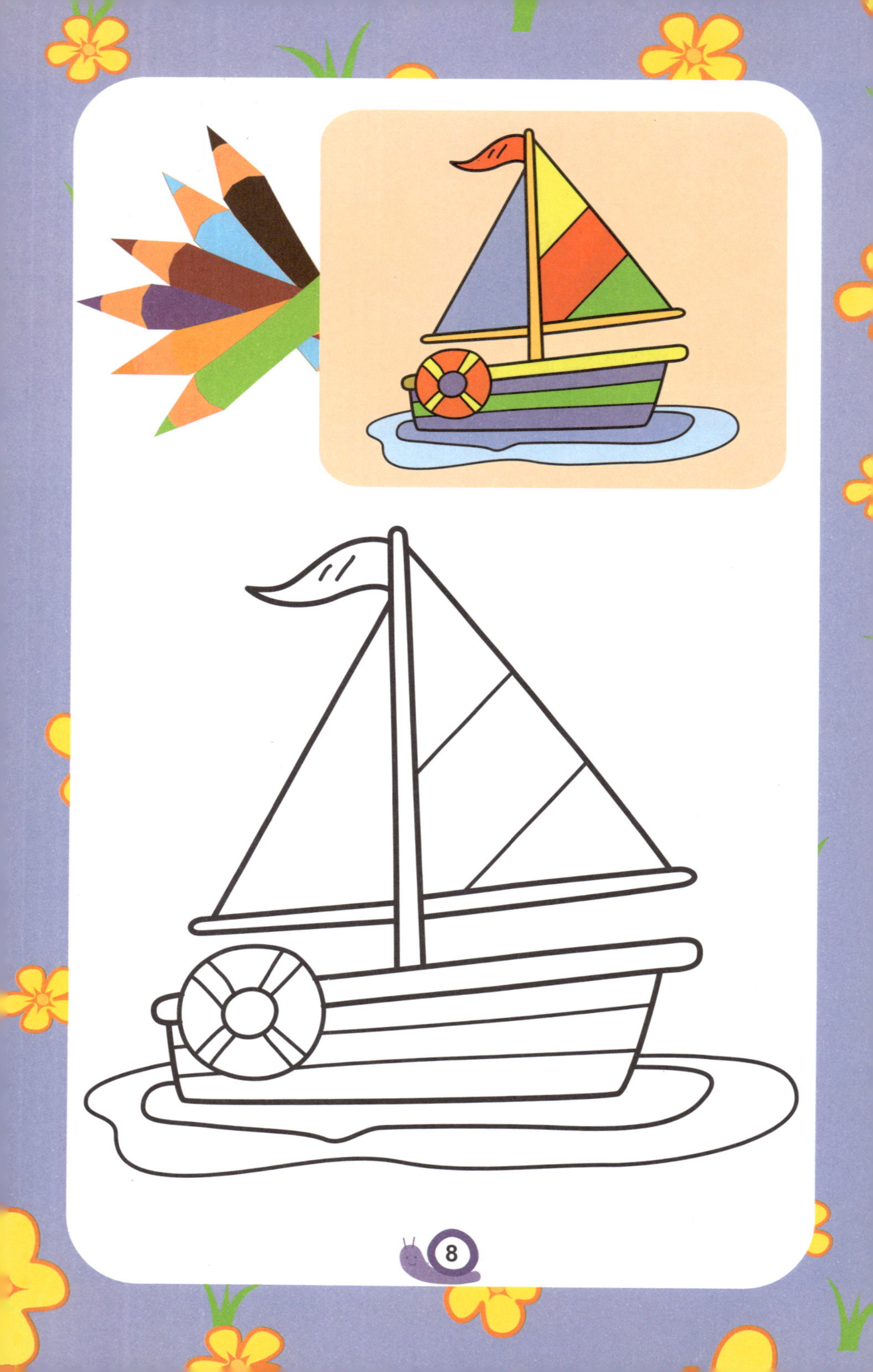

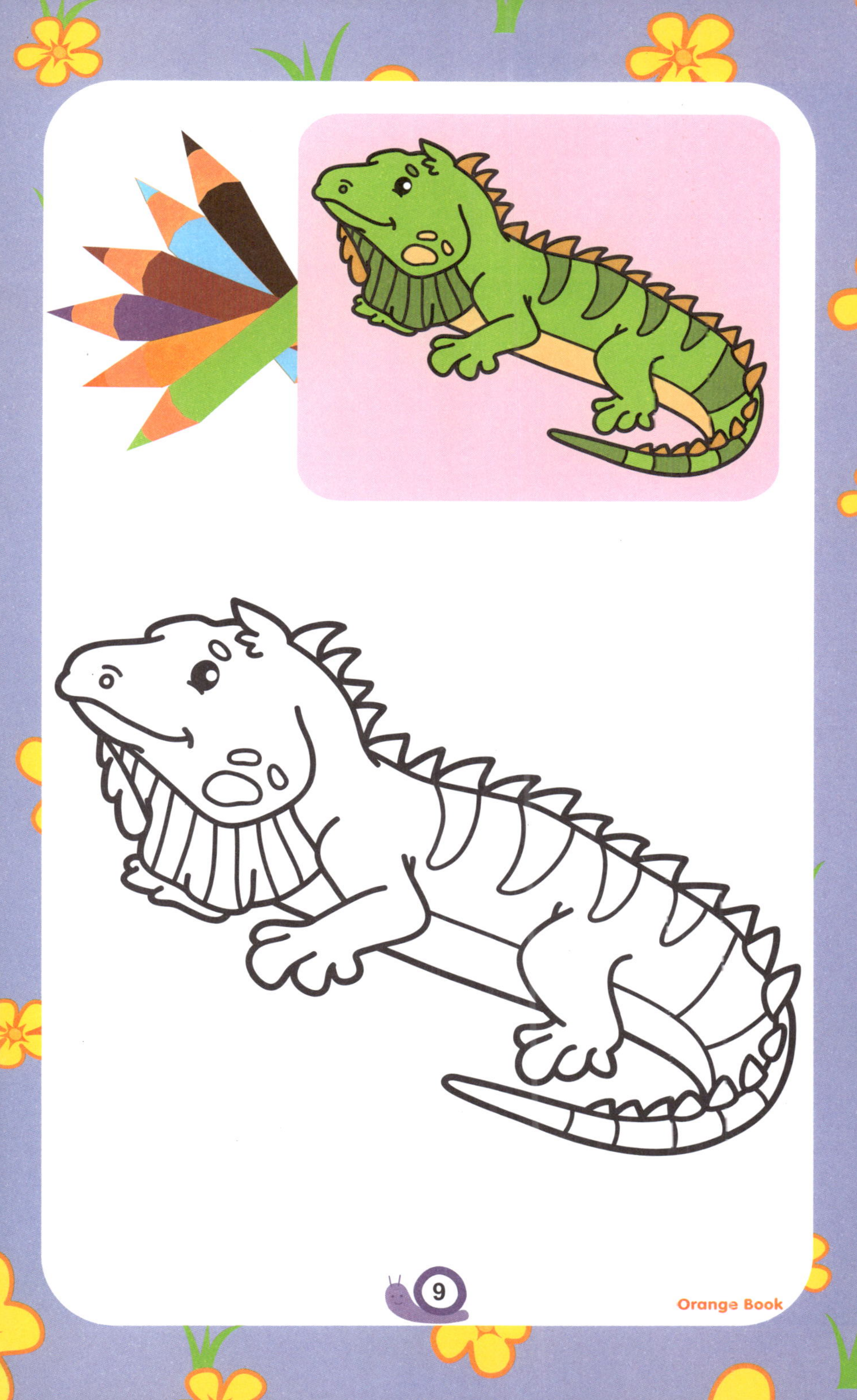

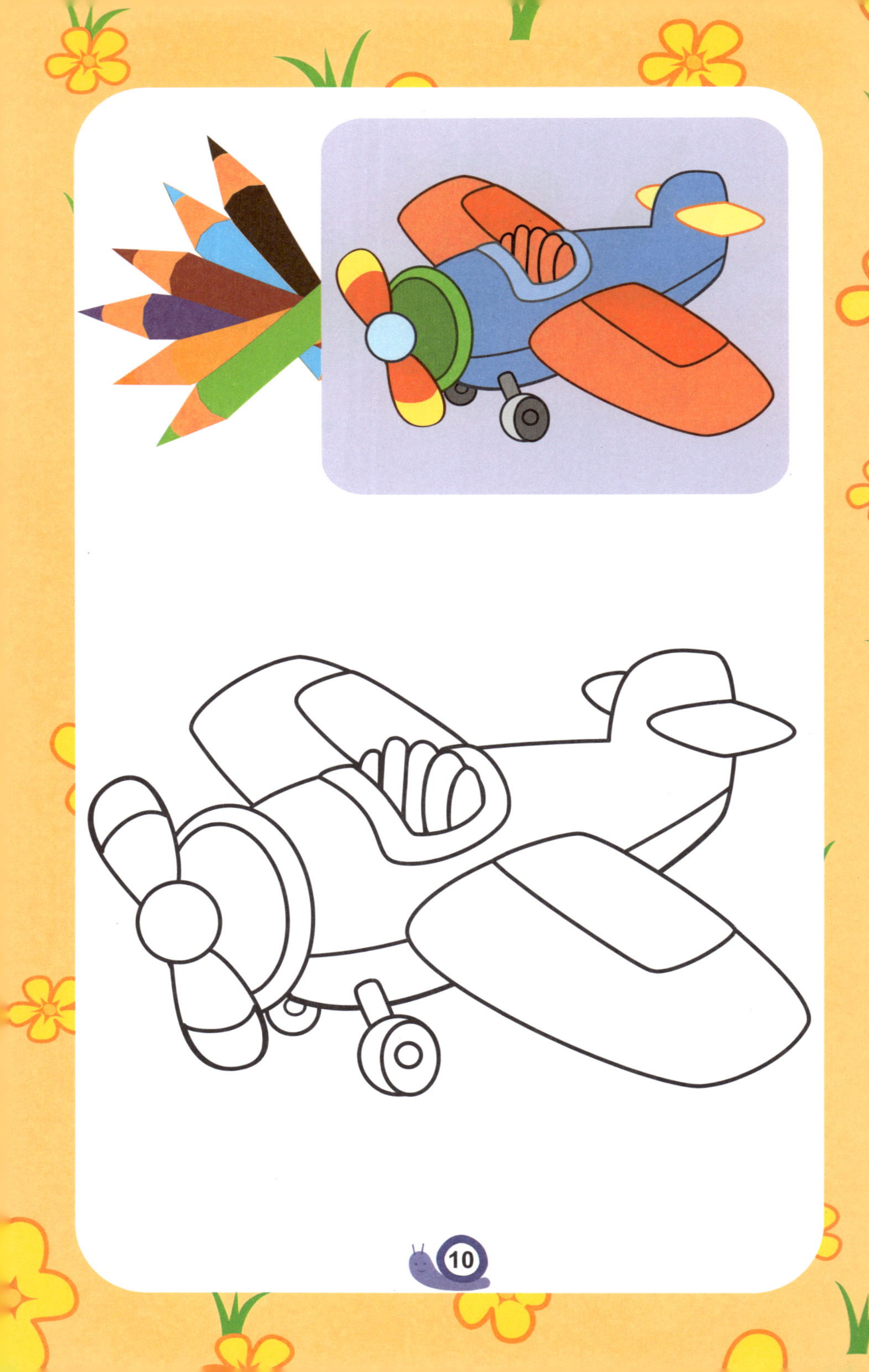

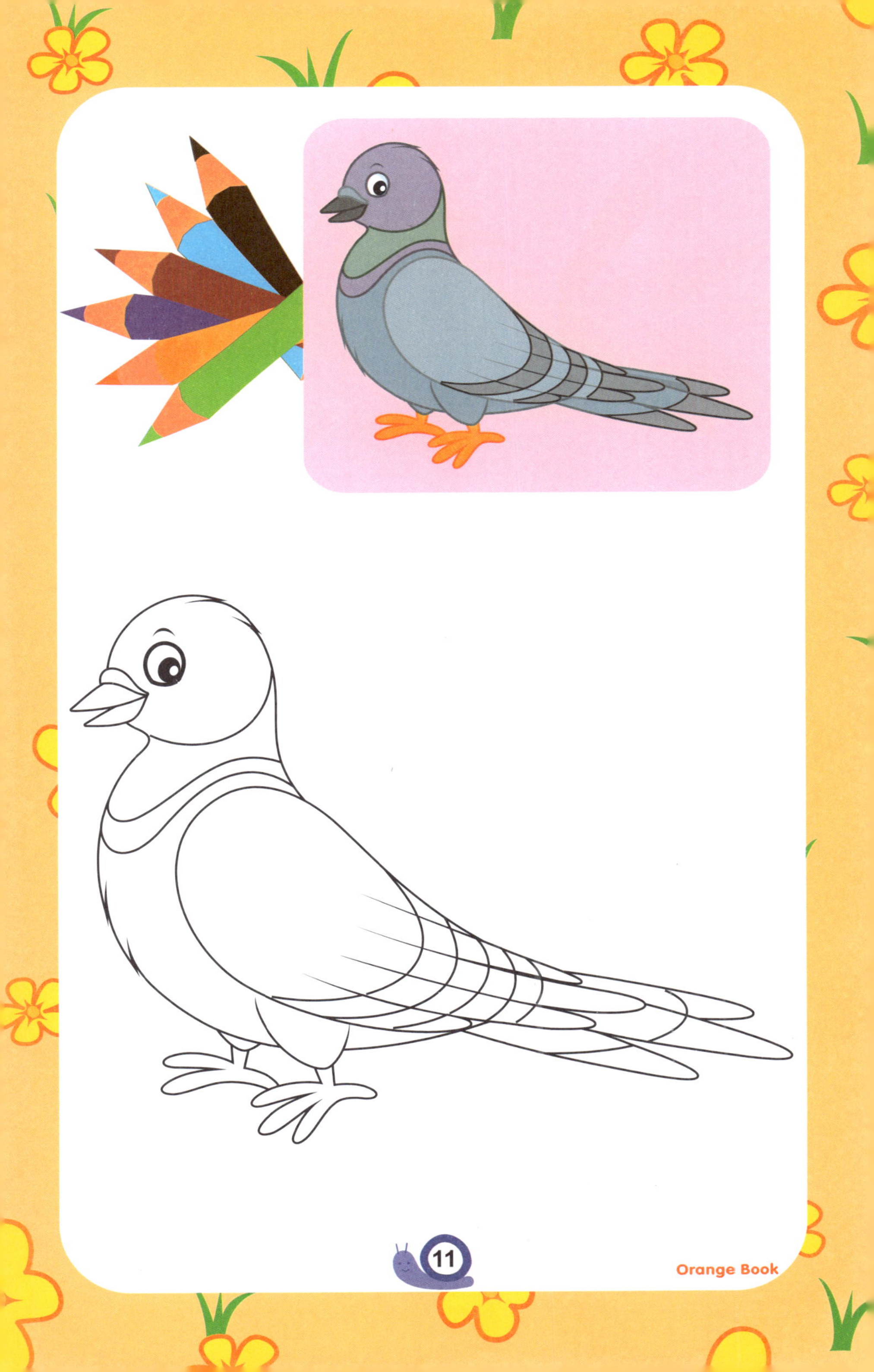

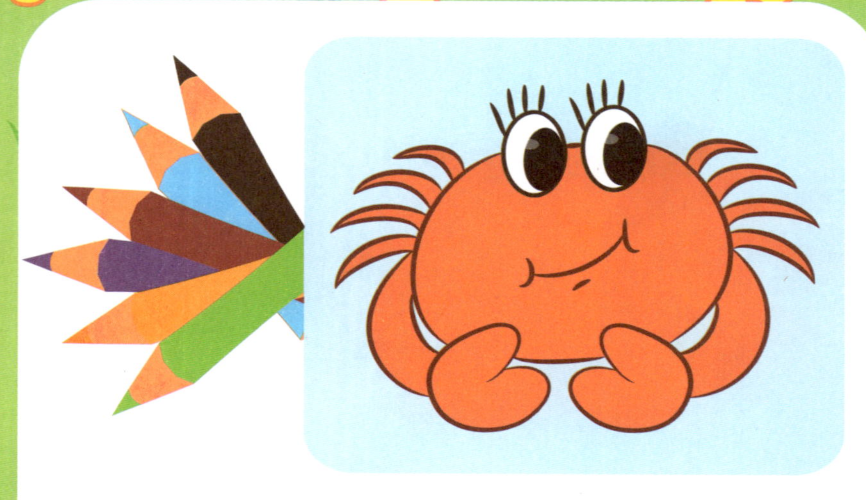

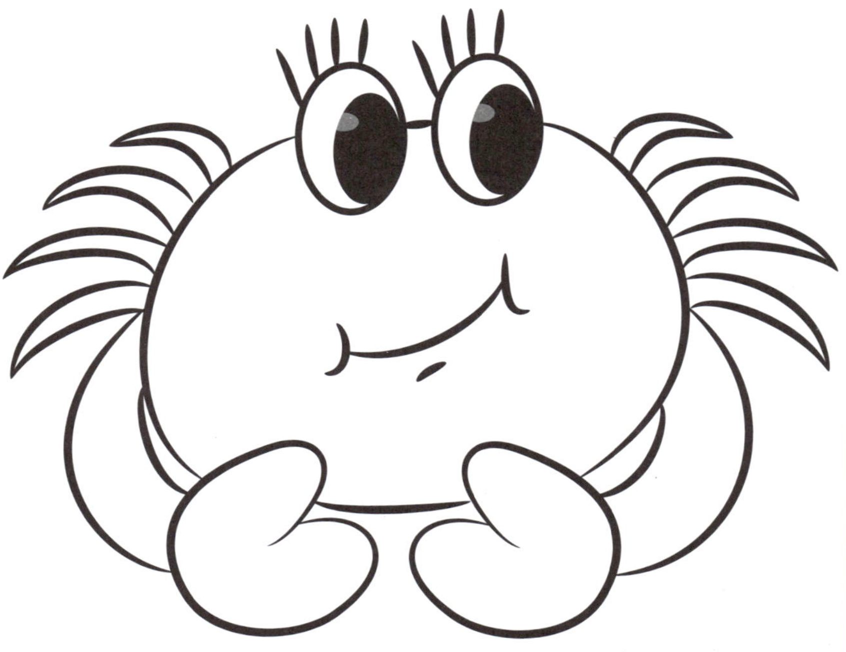

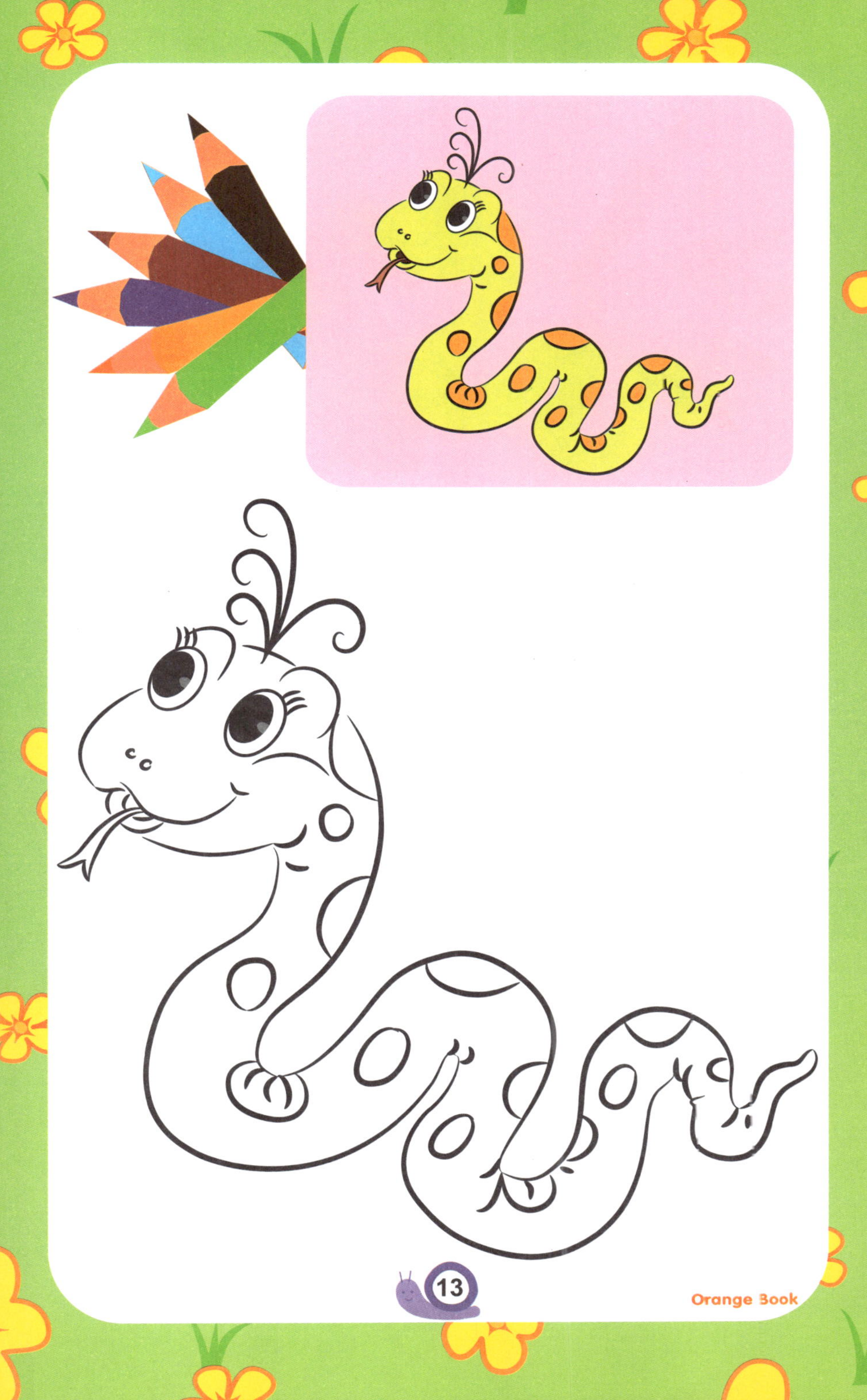

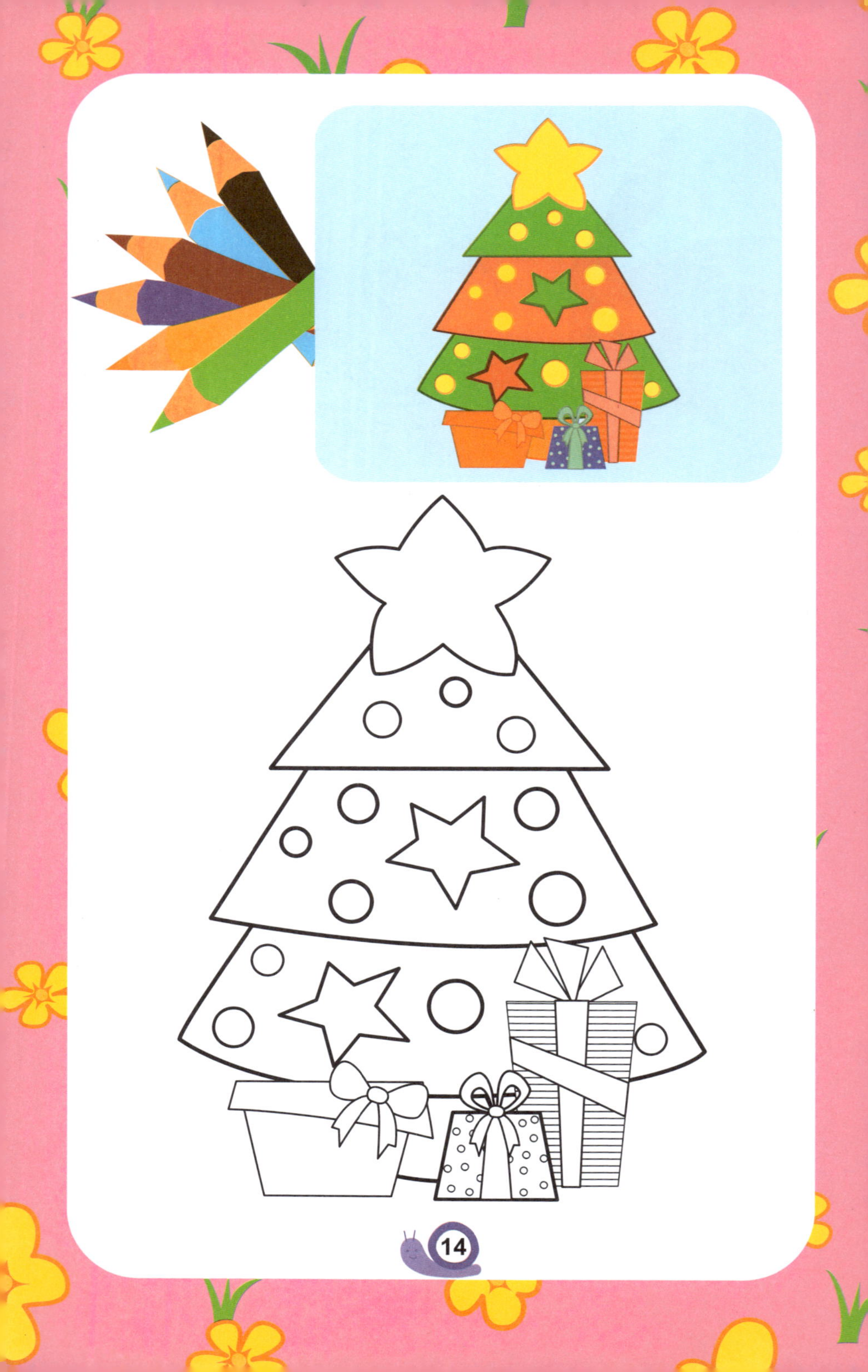

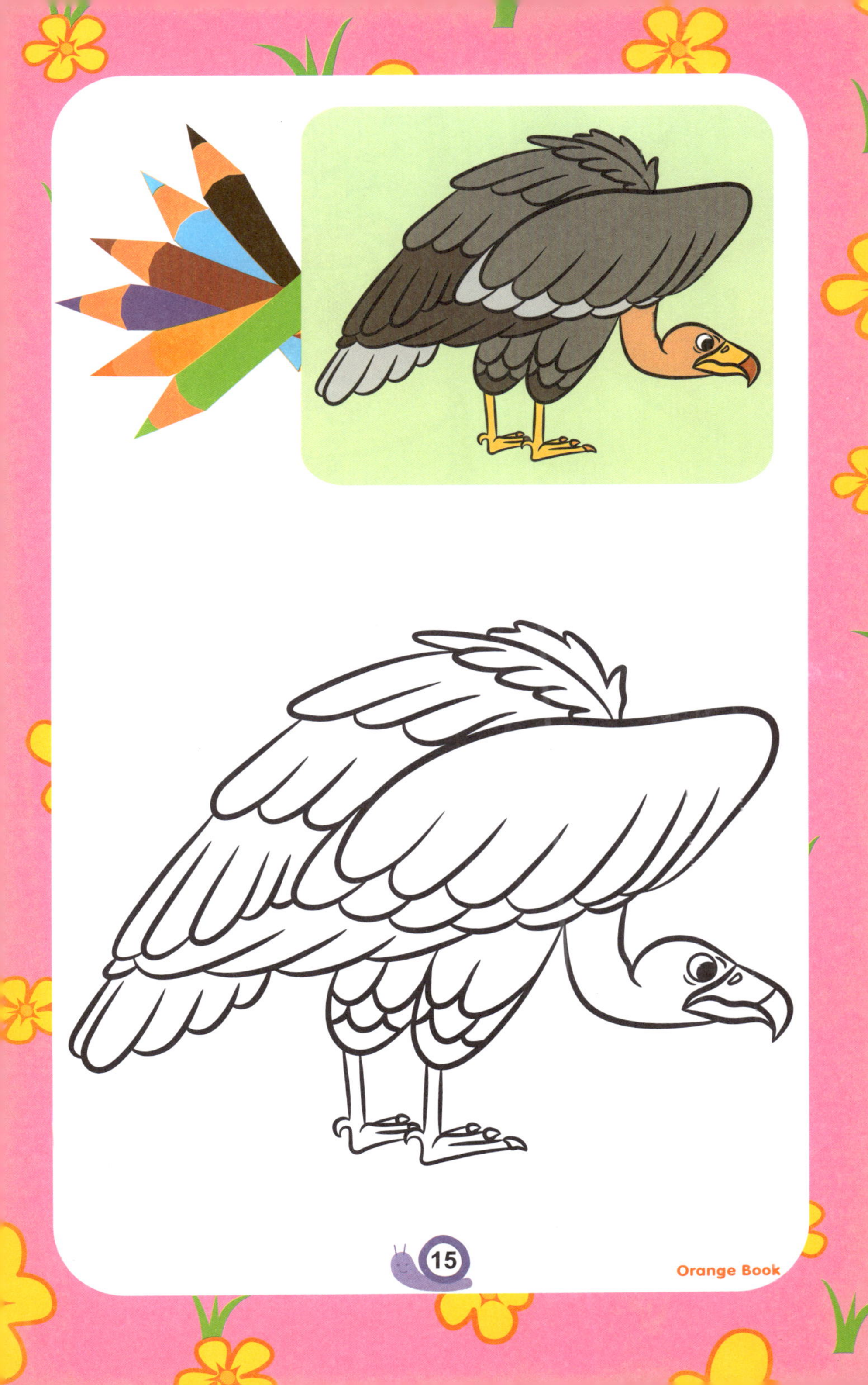

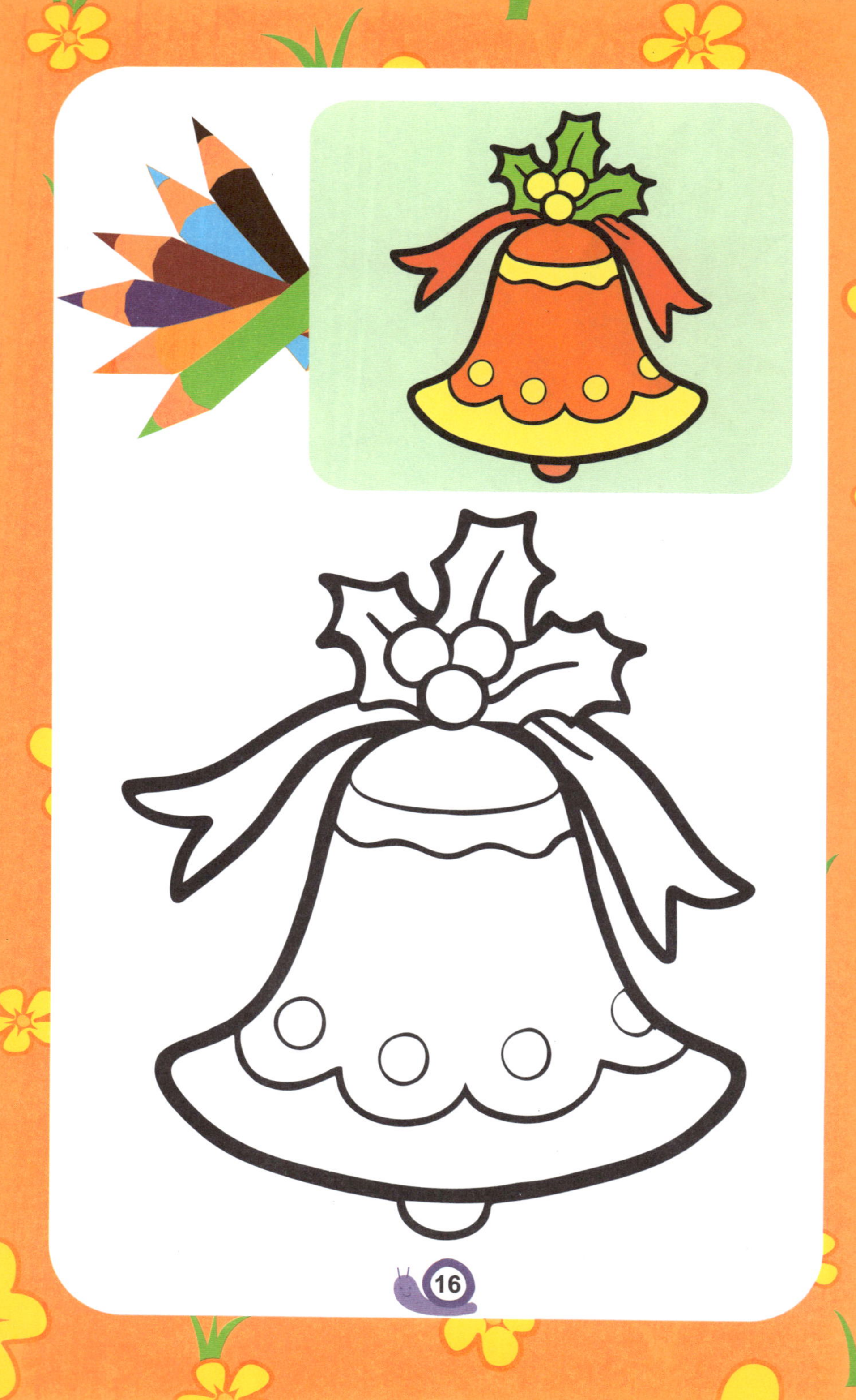